GREAT WHITE SHARK VS. KILLER WHALE

BY THOMAS K. ADAMSON

BELLWETHER MEDIA • MINNEAPOLIS, MN

TM

Torque brims with excitement
perfect for thrill-seekers of all kinds.
Discover daring survival skills, explore
uncharted worlds, and marvel at mighty
engines and extreme sports. In *Torque* books,
anything can happen. Are you ready?

This edition first published in 2020 by Bellwether Media, Inc.

No part of this publication may be reproduced in whole or in part without written
permission of the publisher.
For information regarding permission, write to Bellwether Media, Inc.,
Attention: Permissions Department,
6012 Blue Circle Drive, Minnetonka, MN 55343.

Library of Congress Cataloging-in-Publication Data

Names: Adamson, Thomas K., 1970- author.
Title: Great White Shark vs. Killer Whale / by Thomas K. Adamson.
  Other titles: Great white shark versus killer whale
Description: Minneapolis, MN : Bellwether Media, Inc., 2020. | Series:
  Torque: animal battles | Includes bibliographical references and index.
  | Audience: Ages 7-12 | Audience: Grades 3-7 | Summary: "Amazing
  photography accompanies engaging information about great white sharks
  and killer whales. The combination of high-interest subject matter and
  light text is intended for students in grades 3 through 7"– Provided by publisher.
Identifiers: LCCN 2019030594 (print) | LCCN 2019030595 (ebook) |
  ISBN 9781644871577 (library binding) | ISBN 9781618918376 (ebook)
Subjects: LCSH: White shark–Juvenile literature. | Killer whale–Juvenile literature.
Classification: LCC QL638.95.L3 A33 2020 (print) | LCC QL638.95.L3 (ebook) |
  DDC 597.3/3–dc23
LC record available at https://lccn.loc.gov/2019030594
LC ebook record available at https://lccn.loc.gov/2019030595

Editor: Christina Leaf   Designer: Andrea Schneider

Printed in the United States of America, North Mankato, MN.

TABLE OF CONTENTS

THE COMPETITORS

Two **apex predators** rule the ocean.
The great white shark is well known for its rows
of scary teeth. This huge fish is a feared hunter.

Ocean life also fears the black and white markings of the killer whale. These **mammals** have earned their killer name. Can killer whales and great white sharks share the same water?

KILLER DOLPHIN?

Killer whales are also called orcas. They are not true whales. They are actually large dolphins.

Great white sharks live in all the world's oceans. Their gray backs blend in with rocky or sandy coastal seafloors. Their bellies are white.

Great white sharks have a **streamlined** shape. Their powerful tails provide bursts of speed for taking **prey** by surprise. They eat sea lions, seals, and sea turtles.

GREAT WHITE SHARK PROFILE

0   5 FEET   15 FEET   25 FEET

WEIGHT
UP TO 5,000 POUNDS
(2,268 KILOGRAMS)

LENGTH
UP TO 21 FEET
(6.4 METERS)

HABITAT

ALL OCEANS, ESPECIALLY COOL COASTAL WATERS

GREAT WHITE SHARK RANGE

☐ RANGE

KILLER WHALE PROFILE

```
0        10 FEET      20 FEET      30 FEET
```

LENGTH
33 FEET (10 METERS)

WEIGHT
UP TO 20,000 POUNDS
(9,072 KILOGRAMS)

HABITAT

ALL OCEANS, ESPECIALLY COOL COASTAL WATERS

KILLER WHALE RANGE

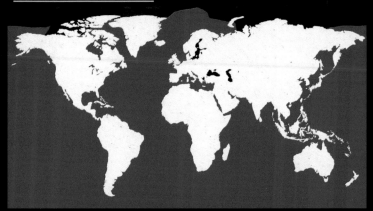

☐ RANGE

NOT A PICKY EATER

An adult killer whale can eat 500 pounds (227 kilograms) of food a day.

Killer whales also live in oceans around the world. They live in **pods** of up to 40. They use **echolocation** to hunt and communicate with one another.

Killer whales work together when hunting. These mammals are not fussy. They eat fish, penguins, seals, sea lions, and even whales!

SECRET WEAPONS

Great white sharks have an incredible sense of smell. They can smell a single drop of blood in 10 billion drops of water. They also have sharp eyesight.

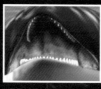

ECHOLOCATION

TEETH

PODS

POD

Killer whales use strength in numbers as a weapon. They hunt in pods. They work together on deadly attacks!

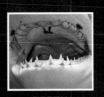
TEETH

LATERAL LINE

SENSE OF SMELL

Great white sharks have a hidden sense. A **lateral line** runs along the sides of the sharks' bodies. These lines can sense **vibrations** in the water. Sharks use it to find prey on the move.

Killer whales have a hidden sense, too. They make sounds for echolocation. The sound waves bounce off objects and back to the mammal. Then they know the prey's distance and size.

GREAT WHITE SHARK TEETH

2.5 INCHES
(6.4 CENTIMETERS)
LONG

Great white sharks have sharp, **serrated** teeth. They cut and rip apart meat. Sharks' teeth fall out often. Rows of teeth replace the ones that fall out.

4 INCHES
(10 CENTIMETERS)
LONG

Killer whales have 40 to 50 rounded teeth. They are made for holding on to prey rather than for chewing. They can be 4 inches (10 centimeters) long.

ATTACK MOVES

Killer whales work together to **herd** fish into a smaller area. This makes it harder for the fish to escape. The killer whales can then eat all they want.

Sharks attack from below. They spot prey on the surface. Then they swim up in a speedy sneak attack and ram into prey.

SCAREDY SHARK

Great white sharks are known to be afraid of killer whales. An orca's scent is often enough to drive great whites away from an area for months.

Killer whales have another nasty move. They raise their tails out of the water. Then they smack down on the prey's head in a mighty karate chop!

Killer whales use smart surprise moves. Their **devious** tactics include splashing to make big waves. The waves knock seals or penguins into the water so the orcas can gobble them up.

Great white sharks take a big bite in the first attack. When the prey is weak, they return to finish it off!

READY, FIGHT!

A great white shark lurks in its favorite hunting area. Suddenly, a pod of killer whales moves in. The shark senses no escape. It opens its mouth to bite.

A killer whale rams the shark! The shark is stunned. Another killer whale flips it upside down. Now the shark cannot move at all! The killer whale pod won this battle!

GLOSSARY

apex predators—animals at the top of the food chain that are not preyed upon by other animals

devious—cunning and deceptive

echolocation—a way of locating objects using reflected sound waves

herd—to move animals together into a group

lateral line—the line along the side of a fish that is sensitive to vibrations

mammals—warm-blooded animals that have backbones and feed their young milk

pods—groups of killer whales

prey—animals that are hunted by other animals for food

serrated—having a blade like that of a saw

streamlined—shaped to move through water easily

vibrations—very rapid back and forth movements

TO LEARN MORE

AT THE LIBRARY

Clausen-Grace, Nicki. *Great White Sharks*. Mankato, Minn.:
Black Rabbit Books, 2019.

Klepeis, Alicia Z. *Orcas on the Hunt*. Minneapolis, Minn.: Lerner
Publications, 2018.

Krajnik, Elizabeth. *Orcas*. New York, N.Y.: PowerKids Press,
2020.

ON THE WEB

FACTSURFER

Factsurfer.com gives you
a safe, fun way to find
more information.

1. Go to www.factsurfer.com

2. Enter "great white shark vs. killer whale" into the
   search box and click 🔍.

3. Select your book cover to see a list of related web sites.

INDEX

The images in this book are reproduced through the courtesy of: ARTYuSTUDIO, front cover (shark); David Pruter, front cover (whale); VisionDive, p. 4; Nature Picture Library/ Alamy Stock Photo, p. 5; Ramon Carretero, pp. 6-7; Arco Images GmbH/ Alamy Stock Photo, pp. 8-9; davidstephens, p. 10; Tory Kallman, p. 11 (whale, weapon 3); Juniors/ SuperStock, pp. 11 (weapon 1), 13; Christian Musat, pp. 11 (weapon 1), 15; Ramon Carretero, p. 12 (shark); wildestanimal, pp. 12 (weapon 1, 3), 20-21 (whales); Alessandro De Maddalena, pp. 12 (weapon 2), 14; Christopher Meder, p. 16 (whale); Leonardo Gonzalez, p. 16 (fish); Stephen Belcher/ Minden Pictures, p. 17; Stephen Lew, p. 18; USO, p. 19; Willyam Bradberry, p. 20; CO Leong, pp. 20-21 (whales).